William Bradford

Governor of Plymouth Colony

Colonial Leaders

Lord Baltimore *English Politician and Colonist*

Benjamin Banneker *American Mathematician and Astronomer*

William Bradford *Governor of Plymouth Colony*

Benjamin Franklin *American Statesman, Scientist, and Writer*

Anne Hutchinson *Religious Leader*

Cotton Mather *Author, Clergyman, and Scholar*

William Penn *Founder of Democracy*

John Smith *English Explorer and Colonist*

Miles Standish *Plymouth Colony Leader*

Peter Stuyvesant *Dutch Military Leader*

Revolutionary War Leaders

Benedict Arnold *Traitor to the Cause*

Nathan Hale *Revolutionary Hero*

Alexander Hamilton *First U.S. Secretary of the Treasury*

Patrick Henry *American Statesman and Speaker*

Thomas Jefferson *Author of the Declaration of Independence*

John Paul Jones *Father of the U.S. Navy*

Thomas Paine *Political Writer*

Paul Revere *American Patriot*

Betsy Ross *American Patriot*

George Washington *First U.S. President*

Colonial Leaders

William Bradford

Governor of Plymouth Colony

Marianne Kendrick Hering

Arthur M. Schlesinger, jr.
Senior Consulting Editor

Chelsea House Publishers

Philadelphia

Produced by Robert Gerson Publisher's Services, Avondale, PA

CHELSEA HOUSE PUBLISHERS
Editor in Chief Stephen Reginald
Production Manager Pamela Loos
Director of Photography Judy L. Hasday
Art Director Sara Davis
Managing Editor James D. Gallagher

Staff for *WILLIAM BRADFORD*
Project Editor Anne Hill
Project Editor/Publishing Coordinator Jim McAvoy
Contributing Editor Amy Handy
Associate Art Director Takeshi Takahashi
Series Design Keith Trego

The Chelsea House World Wide Web address is http://www.chelseahouse.com

First Printing
1 3 5 7 9 8 6 4 2

Library of Congress Cataloging-in-Publication Data

Hering, Marianne.
William Bradford / by Marianne Hering.
    p. cm.— (Colonial leaders)
Includes bibliographical references and index.
Summary: A biography of William Bradford, from his childhood and religious
persecution in England to his years as the first governor of the Plymouth Colony.
ISBN 0-7910-5341-5 (hc); 0-7910-5684-8 (pb)
1. Bradford, William, 1588–1657 Juvenile literature.   2. Pilgrims (New Plymouth
Colony) Biography Juvenile literature.   3. Governors—Massachusetts Biography
Juvenile literature.   4. Massachusetts—History—New Plymouth, 1620–1691 Juve-
nile literature.   5. Plymouth (Mass.) Biography Juvenile literature. [1. Bradford,
William, 1588-1657. 2. Governors.   3. Pilgrims (New Plymouth Colony)
4. Massachusetts—History—New Plymouth, 1620–1691.] I. Title. II. Series.
F68.B8235H47   1999
974.4'02'092—dc21
[B]   99-24006
                                                                  CIP

30652000##30356

> **Publisher's Note:** In Colonial and Revolutionary War America,
> there were no standard rules for spelling, punctuation, capitaliza-
> tion, or grammar. Some of the quotations that appear in the Colo-
> nial Leaders and Revolutionary War Leaders series come from
> original documents and letters written during this time in history.
> Original quotations reflect writing inconsistencies of the period.

Contents

William grew up on a farm with his uncles, but life there was slow and lonely for the young boy who loved to read and reflect.

William Finds a Family

Twelve-year-old William Bradford got out of bed before the sun had a chance to warm the English farmhouse in which he lived. After dressing, he picked up his shoes and carried them to the door. He wanted to be quiet so as not to wake his two slumbering uncles and their families. If they knew where William was going, they would surely try to stop him.

A friend was waiting outside. William put on his sturdy plain leather shoes and hurried away with his friend one Sunday morning in 1602. The Austerfield countryside was full of thick trees, much like Robin Hood's Sherwood Forest not many miles away.

After an eight-mile walk on a twisty dirt road, the boys arrived at the Puritan church in Babworth. They heard preaching that was easy to understand. William and his friend listened to many new ideas. The preacher's words made sense to William. They matched what William had been reading in the Bible.

Before now, William had always gone to an **Anglican** church at Austerfield. He had been baptized there just after he was born in March 1590. Every Sunday the Bradford family would sit in the same **pew** and listen to the same ideas.

Sundays at Babworth were different for William. The Puritan way of thinking excited him, and the church seemed friendlier than the Church of England. William decided he would go back again to listen to the Puritan preacher. He would walk to Babworth every Sunday—even if it made his uncles angry.

William wasn't used to going against the wishes of his uncles. He had lived with them for five years. William's father died when he was just a year old. At age four, he went to live with his grandfather after his mother married again. When he was seven, both his grandfather and mother died. And so William was sent to live with his uncles, Robert and Thomas Bradford.

Life on the Bradford farm wasn't a bad life—if you liked sheep. For years sheep farming had been the family way of life. Every boy in the Bradford family was given a female lamb, or ewe, as soon as he was old enough to care for it. The ewe would be the beginning of the boy's own flock. The Bradfords had a nice house and made a good living. All their friends and neighbors looked up to them. Robert and Thomas Bradford liked their life.

But the problem was that William didn't like shepherding. The life was lonely. He had to go out and watch the sheep all day long with no one to talk to. He loved to read, and there never seemed to be enough books for him to look at. His uncles worked long hours and had no time to give him any attention. William's only sister,

Like the other boys in his family, as soon as he was old enough, William received a lamb to start his own flock.

Alice, lived in a different house. Because he was so lonely, William was often sick. He longed for friends and for something exciting to do.

That Sunday when he got home, his uncles asked where he had gone. Why hadn't William been at the family church? When William told them he went to a Puritan church, his uncles got very angry. They didn't agree with the way the **Puritans** worshiped, and they reminded William that his place was with the Bradfords in the family pew.

But William didn't listen to them. He listened to his heart and to what he thought the Bible said. The next Sunday he went back to the Puritan church and enjoyed the simple service. He went again and again.

Four years later, William Bradford attended other secret church services. To get to the house where the meeting was held, he may have hid behind some thick bushes near the **moat**. The moat surrounded a large, brick house that was at least a 1,000 years old. But before he went close to the house, William would check to make sure no one from the road was watching him.

Then, when all was quiet, he quickly stepped across the wooden bridge to the stone steps. These he followed to the heavy, dark oak door. He knocked, hoping someone would answer quickly. William didn't want anyone to see him go inside. If someone from town noticed him, everyone in the house could be arrested.

The door creaked open and William was welcomed inside by his friend, Mr. Brewster. Other Puritan friends sat in a comfortable room in the Brewsters' house. This Lord's day, the small group was separating from the Puritans and the Church of England. To make it official, they made up a membership agreement. William Bradford signed the list. The group was to become known as the Separatists from Scrooby.

William probably learned to read at a school three miles from his home. Foxe's *Book of Martyrs* was one of his favorite books. Like the Bible, it shaped a lot of his ideas. It tells about brave people who were tortured or killed, because they believed in religious ideas that were different than Queen Mary's.

Starting a new group was the only way the Separatists could worship freely. Just three years before, in 1603, England got a new king. His name was King James. The Puritans hoped this king would be open to new ideas, but the king liked the old ways. He didn't like fancy ideas about how to change the church, so he didn't like the Puritans. King James made a law that said the Puritans couldn't meet by themselves. As part of the Church of England, he wanted them to act like everybody else. Most of all, he wanted them to be quiet. He said, "I will put down this Puritan devil even if it cost me my crown."

And King James did his best to destroy the Puritans. Many people who said or wrote things about how to change the Church of England were put in prison. Some were killed. Many were forced from their homes and all their money was taken.

The king was out to destroy the Puritan movement, and many Puritans lost hope that the Church of England would ever be changed. One of those people was Mr. Brewster. He was a kind, gentle man. William Bradford wrote that Mr. Brewster was "of a very cherful spirite, very sociable & pleasante amongst his friends." He loaned William books and let him stay at his 40-room house. Mr. Brewster also had a good job. He was in charge of the mail that came through Scrooby, and he kept horses ready in case a king's servant needed one.

Mr. Brewster didn't like what King James was doing. He wanted to worship God the way he thought the Bible told him to. He didn't want to wait for the king to change his mind. So Mr. Brewster and a few other men decided to start the new gathering in Scrooby.

At the Scrooby meetings, William Bradford felt welcome. The people were like his family. He was allowed to ask questions and openly discuss what was written in the Bible. The people chose their own leaders from among themselves. In the Church of England, no one was allowed

King James I wanted to punish anyone who did not belong to the Church of England.

to ask questions at all. The men in charge were appointed by the king, not by the people.

For about a year, the Scrooby Separatists met in secret without trouble. At first William's uncles didn't say anything about the Separatist meetings. Then King James made another new law, one that said every man in England had to go the Church of England, or he would be put in jail.

William's uncles began to express their concern. They again warned him about the Separatists, and told him that his place was with the Bradfords in the Church of England. They even threatened to kick him out of the house if he didn't obey.

But William wouldn't change his mind. He kept listening to his heart and doing what he believed the Bible said. He packed up his few things and went to live with Mr. Brewster and his family.

Soon, not only the king wanted to stop the Separatists, but folks all around England grew to hate them. People wrote untrue stories about the

Separatists and tried to make them seem like bad people. Many Englishmen believed the lies.

The king's men took away land and farm animals from the Separatists. Many people were arrested. All over England, Separatists like the ones from Scrooby were being hunted out and tossed in jail. Nowhere in England did the Separatists feel safe.

One day Mr. Brewster was arrested. He had to tell a high court about the meetings at Scrooby. The court made him pay a huge fine and then let him go. The court also warned him to stop the meetings and to stop talking about starting new churches with new ideas.

Yet Mr. Brewster didn't stop talking. He got new ideas. He thought the Scrooby group should get away from the king. They decided they would move to a different country: Holland.

Like William Bradford, the Separatists had to leave their home because of what they believed.

Seeking relief from the religious persecution they were facing in England, the Separatists wanted to move to Holland. Here, they hoped to find the freedom to worship as they chose.

Holland Days

One of the king's officials held a sturdy knife. He waved the dagger in the air. The man wanted all the Separatists to be searched to the skin. When it was William Bradford's turn, he unbuttoned his plain shirt. After roughly searching the teenager the officer turned to the next man on the small boat. William wasn't worried about himself; he had no money for the officials to take. But many of his Scrooby friends had everything they owned with them.

He looked across the water at the sailing ship that was supposed to be taking the group of Separatists to Holland. After William and his friends had boarded with all their household goods, the captain of the ship tricked them. He set a trap for the Separatists. He planned to turn them over to the king's men. He never planned to take them to Holland at all.

Instead, William and the other men were forced onto small boats, the women onto others. They watched as king's officials and searchers looked through their bags and trunks. They took books, money, and other valuable things.

Even the women were searched beneath their clothes to see if they were hiding gold or money. When they were through, the band of king's men and their helpers rounded up the scared Separatists. William Bradford later wrote that the searchers and officials brought them to town "and made a spectacle of them to the [crowds] that came flocking on all sides to see them."

Next the sad group was thrown into jail. William Bradford sat on the dirt floor in his cell. He wondered if he would ever see outside again, let alone Holland. The lad had a long time to think that winter of 1607. If he ever got out of prison, he had to have plans. Was moving to Holland a good idea? Would he ever learn the language? Could he find a job? Did he really want to leave his part of the Bradford farm behind forever?

William knew Holland was the only place in Europe where he and his friends could find religious peace. In Holland there was no king to tell them which church to attend. The Separatists could worship God in the way they believed was right. To William Bradford and his friends, this freedom meant more than money, their country, their trades, and their family ties. Many were even willing to die for **religious freedom**. Teenage William was brave and firm about what he believed was right. He had already been sent to jail because of his desire for freedom. He would not give up. He would get to Holland one way or another.

A month later, the officials let William and most of the other Separatists go. Only seven of the group remained in jail. But being out of jail was hardly any better than being in jail. The Scrooby friends had already sold their homes, and all their money had been taken. They were in a foreign **port** city, far from their homeland. To add to their troubles, their leaders were still locked up.

One by one the families managed to find places to stay. Some moved in with Separatists who weren't going to Holland. Some stayed with relatives in other cities. William stayed near Mr. Brewster and his family. Mrs. Brewster had just had a baby. The Brewsters named her Fear because that's what they felt during those months in England.

In spring of 1808 the Scrooby folks tried again to get to Holland in one big group. This time the men had to walk 40 miles to the ship. They wanted to be well hidden from the king's officials. The women went to meet the ship on a flat boat. It got stuck in the mud and the women and children couldn't get to the ship. A few men did get on the ship, and some were left on shore.

From the ship, the men and the captain saw a great mob of men with guns and knives coming toward the water. The captain sailed out to sea. William Bradford, who had not gone on the ship, stayed on shore to help the women. Once again the Separatists were captured, dragged through the streets, and sent to court. Then the officials didn't know what to do with them, so they let the Separatists go. According to William, the officials were "glad to be rid of them on any terms; for all were wearied and tired of them."

Months later, in August 1608, William stood on a different ship and could finally see Holland, his new home. At the dock in Middleburg, he waited his turn to step off the ship. His heart swelled with joy knowing that in this country he would be free to worship the way he desired. He was one of the last Scrooby Separatists to be sent over. Instead of traveling in a large group this time, the Separatists had sailed to Holland individually or in small groups.

Finally, after many setbacks, the Separatists managed to reach Holland. William lived with the Brewsters in Amsterdam, a city of many canals.

But before he could find his friends, a group of Dutch officials stopped 18-year-old William. Had someone told them he was fleeing England? Would he be arrested and sent back to England for being a Separatist?

They questioned him in English, asking things like what he was doing there, whether he had friends there who knew him, and how the officials could be sure who he really was. The questions came fast. William answered them as best as he could. He sounded educated, well-mannered, and bright.

Then the group of Dutch men gathered to talk. William wished he knew what they were saying. He wanted to know why he was being stopped from entering Holland. After all the work to get to Holland, he didn't want to be sent back to England.

Finally the men motioned for him to go. Someone told them that young Bradford looked like a man who was running away from England. The man said William was a thief. But the

Dutch officials decided that the man was wrong. They let him go.

William nodded his head and stammered his thanks. He ran down the ramp of the ship to the dock, thankful to be on dry ground. Thankful, indeed, to be in free Holland.

About a year later, William walked toward the tiny house he shared with the Brewsters. He was leaving the shop where he worked at a **loom** making silk. The dark shadows of the buildings made the city seem unhappy and crowded. William wondered if he would ever get used to the busy city. Amsterdam was large, like London, and strange compared to the farmlands William knew so well.

Some businessmen loaned the Separatists money to travel to America. In return they wanted work from all the Pilgrims for seven years. That was too much time for some Separatists, and they decided not to go. But for William, seven years was not too long to work for free land and free worship.

Even though the small group from Scrooby found help and friends quickly, they were still unhappy in Amsterdam. No matter how hard they worked, they didn't have enough money. Many days they went hungry. Several other English Separatists lived in Amsterdam, but they had problems in their churches. The 20 or so Scrooby friends decided to move to Leyden. About 80 other English Separatists decided to go with them.

Moving to Leyden was fine with William. There was nothing special in Amsterdam for him—except Dorothy May. She was a pretty girl in her early teens, but she was too young to be married. Also, William didn't have his own house or a good job. He didn't have a way to support Dorothy May. He would have to wait to marry her.

Many good things happened in Leyden for William. He got some of the Bradford money from England and he bought a house. His job as a weaver was going well. He had enough money to marry. So when she was 16, Dorothy May and William got married. Soon they had a little boy named John.

William became a weaver in Holland and spent his days at a loom weaving silk, just like the man in this present-day photo.

But the Separatists were afraid. Holland was going to go to war with Spain. If Spain won, a king or queen would rule Holland. They would not be free anymore. No one wanted to keep their church a secret, so they decided to go somewhere far away where they wouldn't be bothered. America seemed to be the perfect place.

And so once again, William left his home to find peace in a new land.

The *Mayflower* set sail from England in 1620 with more than 100 passengers aboard, including the Bradfords. A modern replica shows what the ship looked like.

Troubled
Waters

On September 6, 1620, William and
Dorothy Bradford sailed away from their
old life toward America. They also left their son,
John, behind in Holland with some friends. While
sad to leave him behind, they knew the trip would
be hard. They didn't know when they would ever
see their son again.

The wind was good and strong. It made the
Mayflower sail fast. It also made the ship rock, and
most of the passengers got seasick.

Below deck, William Bradford and his wife had
to share sleeping quarters with many other people
on the *Mayflower*. There was no room for anyone to

be alone. The mix of passengers made for strange roommates. The 40 or so Separatists, or **"Saints,"** were only a part of a large crowd. Other pioneers from England, or **"Strangers,"** just wanted a new place to live; they were not concerned about religious freedom. Together the group became known as the Pilgrims. They all had to get along if they were going to make new lives in the New World.

The Pilgrims had to share their space with the sailors, too. One sailor was especially rude and told the sick Pilgrims they would die onboard the ship. But one day, the sailor himself got sick and soon died. William thought that the sailor's death showed that God was protecting the Pilgrims.

Other people onboard were helpful. William made friends with them. The Pilgrims didn't have much to do besides talk. As they shared their dried fish, beer, and hard crackers at mealtimes, people got to know one another. William grew to like many of the Strangers, and he became popular as well.

After more than two months at sea under very uncomfortable conditions, the Pilgrims were glad to reach land. They first set foot on the coast of what would later become Massachusetts.

After two months at sea, the *Mayflower* finally stopped at Cape Cod, a sandy spot on the coast of modern-day Massachusetts.

No one was allowed off the ship even though they had reached land. The men, William Bradford included, had business to do first. They got together and talked about how they would all get along. In the New World, there were no old laws. Some people said they should do whatever they wanted. Others said that they should follow God's rules. The men finally decided that they would vote for a leader and have just and equal laws. These ideas were very different from those in England. The men wrote the new ideas down on a piece of paper and signed their names to this special agreement, called the Mayflower **Compact**. Finally the Pilgrim men voted for a governor. They chose a man named John Carver.

Once on land the Saints dropped to their knees and thanked God for keeping them safe. One of the first things the women did when they got off the ship was to wash their very dirty clothes.

After months of seeing nothing besides gray water, Dorothy Bradford looked at the new land.

The Saints and the Strangers worked together
to write the Mayflower Compact so they
would have laws to live by in their new home.

Most of the Pilgrims signed the compact. William's name is at the upper left.

It was full of trees, bushes, and rocks. It was not a bit like Holland, where she had grown up. Cape Cod may have looked wild and scary to her, as it did to many other Europeans. But William liked the feel of it. He could sense the freedom of the land in his heart. He was finally at home.

A few days later, William got to look at the land from upside down. He had stepped into a deer trap by accident. Strong ropes made by **Native Americans** held his ankles. The bushes appeared thicker and the ground certainly seemed harder. Hanging upside down in a tree, even the trees looked different. They seemed much taller. William dangled and wiggled. He begged his nearby friends to cut him free. They did, though the story about it was told for many years afterward.

Hours before William's mishap, he couldn't wait to explore the land. With Captain Miles Standish as their leader, 16 of the Pilgrim men set out to find wood, water, and a good place to live. A good place would have fresh water and an area to plant crops. It would be far away from Native Americans but close to the shore so ships could easily come and go. Cape Cod didn't have all of these things.

All the men carried **muskets** and knives. They knew that Native Americans lived in the area, and the Pilgrims did not know if they were friendly. No sooner had the Pilgrim explorers walked part way up the beach when they saw six Native Americans and a dog. Quickly, the Native Americans turned and ran away. They were fast. The Pilgrims tried to catch them but couldn't run as quickly. Soon the Native Americans were out of sight.

Dangers like being caught in the trap didn't stop William from exploring. He went on several trips to discover what was in the New World. On one trip the Pilgrim men brought back a lot of corn that the Native Americans had buried. On another trip the Pilgrim explorers had to journey in the snow. Winter was coming quickly, and they needed shelter. They searched for weeks but did not find a good spot to settle. The Pilgrims decided to look at a different place altogether. William was one of 10 men who sailed a small boat along the coast. In freezing rain and after many adventures, the boat landed at Plymouth. There the Pilgrim explorers found everything they were looking for in a home: fresh water, a good port, and cleared land.

Happy to spread the good news, the men returned to the *Mayflower.* William rushed to tell Dorothy she would have a good place to live. He

Led by Captain Miles Standish, the Pilgrims explored the new land, hoping to find food, a plentiful water supply, and a good place to build homes.

hoped she would like Plymouth better than the thick forests around Cape Cod.

But Dorothy wasn't there. She had fallen overboard in the shallow seawater. No one was there to save her, and she had drowned.

William had found a new home, but now he had no one to share it with.

Samoset was the first contact the Pilgrims had with the Native Americans, but not all the run-ins with Indians were friendly.

Dangers in
the Night

On Christmas Day 1620, there were no gifts or special treats for the Pilgrims. Jesus's birth is told about in the New Testament, but the Christmas tradition is not. For that reason the Saints did not celebrate the holiday. Instead they worked, and the Strangers worked with them. William and the rest of the men cut down trees and began to make shelter out of dirt, grass, and branches.

All through the winter, the rain and snow kept coming. The Pilgrims could not keep dry on the *Mayflower* or in their little huts. During the hard weeks of building, many Pilgrims got sick. The sick Pilgrims stayed in the first house that was finished.

The Pilgrims called it the common house, but they had to use it as a hospital.

William was one of the sick people. He was ill from the loss of Dorothy, and his hip hurt so much he could not stand up. He was taken to the common house, where he spent the night with many others.

Loud screams awoke William one night. The roof of the hospital was ablaze. Bundles of burning straw fell down on the sleeping sick people.

There were several barrels of gunpowder all around the common house. Next to them stood loaded muskets. If even one spark landed on them, the hospital would blow up! William had to hurry to get away.

Here are some **myths** about the Pilgrims, followed by the truths:

- *Pilgrims always wore black.* Except on the Lord's day, the Pilgrims wore brighter colors like reddish-brown and green.
- *The Pilgrims lived in log houses.* Their houses were built of clay and planks. The roofs were made of leaves of grass.
- *The Pilgrims ate turkey, cranberries, and pumpkin pie on the first Thanksgiving.* The meal served was mainly shellfish, deer meat, eels, and salad.

Every able Pilgrim quickly moved the gunpowder and muskets out of danger. They dragged the sick people outside. William was well enough to stand up, but he couldn't help much. From outside, he watched the common house burn.

Almost everything he owned was inside. Once the fire was out, William had very little left. Now he had no wife, and very few belongings. But he still had something he felt was worth a lot: his belief that God would take care of him.

Months later, the settlers at Plymouth had homes. But only half the Pilgrims were left to live in them. About 50 people died that first winter. Because there were so few Pilgrims, they were afraid the Native Americans would attack them. The Pilgrim men had to make plans to protect themselves.

At a meeting where they were talking about how to keep the Indians away, William looked up and saw one. They were too late! A bold and brave Native American was standing right there. He had walked right into the middle of the Pilgrims' homes. He had long hair down his back and he carried a bow and many arrows.

Before the Pilgrim men could jump up and fight, the Native American said, "Welcome."

Welcome! A kind English word. Where had this Indian learned it? What were the Pilgrims to do now?

The Native American called himself Samoset. He liked the Englishmen so much he didn't go home that night. He wanted to stay at the settlement. The frightened Pilgrims kept guard over him while he slept, just in case he might harm them in the middle of the night.

Over the next few days, Samoset brought many Native American friends to visit the Pilgrims. Two important guests were Squanto and the chief, Massasoit.

Squanto, like Samoset, had been captured as a slave and taken to England for a time. He knew English and helped the Pilgrims talk to

Chief Massasoit met with the governor of
Plymouth colony, John Carver, and together
they worked out a peace treaty.

other Native Americans. Governor Carver made friends with Chief Massasoit through Squanto. Soon whole families of Native Americans wanted to be friends. They dropped in at Plymouth and ate a lot of food. The Pilgrims were afraid that their new friends would eat all the food supplies, but the chief soon put an end to the Indians' habit when the Pilgrims told him the problem.

When Squanto came to visit, he did more than eat. He moved in with the Pilgrims; he most likely lived in the same house with William Bradford. Squanto soon became William's good friend. And then William felt sure that God was indeed helping the Pilgrims. William later wrote that Squanto was "a special instrument sent of God for their good." Squanto taught them how to plant food, how to get along with the Native American tribes, and how to survive in the cold. Without Squanto, all the Pilgrims probably would have died.

Even though they had Squanto, many Pilgrims still suffered and some died. In April 1621

The Indians became very friendly with the Pilgrims and enjoyed sharing their food. William Bradford is the man on the left wearing the hat and holding the cup.

the Pilgrims had a particularly sad funeral. Governor John Carver had died. One minute he was farming a field, the next he was holding his head in pain. He died quickly, and was buried in "the best manner possible," according to William. As was their custom, at the end of the funeral, the Pilgrims who had muskets fired into the sky to show respect for the dead.

The Pilgrims had lost a governor, but they soon found a new one. The men voted that William Bradford would guide them. William prayed that God in turn would guide him.

And indeed, from April to October, the Pilgrims were blessed. They finished building all the houses they needed. They traded with the Native Americans for many beaver pelts to send

This is part of the treaty the Pilgrims had with Massasoit's people:
- They would not hurt or steal from each other.
- They would hand enemies over to each other.
- They would help each other if outsiders attacked.
- When the Indians came to Plymouth, they would leave their bows and arrows behind.

back to England. Fish from the sea were caught and given to each family. In the fall wild birds landed on nearby lakes and ponds, and the Pilgrims captured many of them. The corn that Squanto had taught them how to plant came up rich and colorful in shades of red, blue, and yellow.

Squanto taught the Pilgrims how to grow corn and they raised a successful crop that grew in beautiful colors.

William was thankful to God and wanted to do something special. He remembered a custom the people celebrated in Holland in October. And even though the Saints wouldn't celebrate Christmas, they still liked to have a good time. So William declared a holiday of thanksgiving to God and invited Chief Massasoit.

Even though the first Thanksgiving didn't feature turkey and stuffing like we expect today, it did begin the tradition of giving thanks with friends and family.

On the special day, Massasoit did come. And he brought 90 hungry friends. The Pilgrims did not know what to do with the hungry braves, but the chief did. He sent them out to catch more food; the braves soon came back with five deer.

They had enough food for the holiday to last three days. Ten Pilgrim women cooked and served the feast. The Native Americans and the Pilgrim men played games of skill. The Pilgrims showed off their muskets, while the Native Americans showed off their strength. The two groups became even better friends after that first Thanksgiving holiday.

The Pilgrims became good friends with
Chief Massasoit's tribe and they helped
each other, but not all the Native Americans
were glad to have the Pilgrims living there.

A Ship, a Snakeskin, and a Secret

Almost a year after the *Mayflower* sailed into Cape Cod, an Indian came running into the Plymouth settlement, yelling that a ship was coming.

At first William didn't know what to do. He could not be sure that the people on the ship were friendly.

As governor, William could not take any chances. He had to protect the Pilgrims and their homes. He planned to attack if the ship carried any enemies. All the Pilgrims working outside were called to come to the settlement. Each man and older boy took his musket to the shore and waited for the ship. The little army was ready.

When the ship came near shore, the Pilgrims were excited. It was from England. The people on board were friends–maybe they were even family members. All the Pilgrims dropped their muskets as they raced to talk to the first man who got off the ship, which was named the *Fortune.*

Robert Cushman had stayed behind in England because the *Mayflower* didn't have room for everyone. The businessmen who had paid for the Pilgrim's journey on the *Mayflower* sent Mr. Cushman.

Mr. Cushman would help the Pilgrims pay back the businessmen. Before the *Fortune* sailed back to England, the Pilgrims loaded it with beaver and otter skins as well as special wood that had been prepared to make barrels. The cargo would pay off half their bill.

But Mr. Cushman did not plan to take things and leave nothing. He brought with him 34 more people who stayed at Plymouth. One of them was Mr. Brewster's oldest son. None of the newcomers had extra clothes, blankets, kitchen equipment, or tools. They had not brought any extra food–not even a biscuit. But they did bring empty stomachs.

William was happy for the people. But he was not happy about having to feed them. Over the next cold months, the Pilgrims would have to share their food. Each person would receive a half-portion. They would be hungry, but they would not starve.

The *Fortune* brought another thing that made William especially happy. It was a paper that said the Pilgrims could own land and make laws in Plymouth. William Bradford was now a legal governor, and his decisions would mean something even in faraway England. But soon William had big troubles right nearby.

An unknown Native American visitor stopped by Plymouth. He was not one of Massasoit's braves. He did not want to come to a feast or spend the night. The Indian came to bring something: a bunch of arrows with a long snakeskin wrapped around it. Squanto told William that this meant war.

Governor Bradford quickly decided what to do. He sent back the snakeskin to the enemy Native Americans, but first he filled it with bullets. William also sent a message saying that if a war was to happen, they would be prepared.

During the next months, the Pilgrims built a strong wall around the settlement. The gates were guarded all the time and locked at night. William and Captain Standish put the men into four fighting groups. William was the leader of one group. In this way, the Pilgrims were ready to fight or put out fires in case of an attack.

William wrote that finishing the wall "was accomplished very cheerfully, and the town was enclosed by the beginning of March, each family having a pretty garden plot." The enemy tribe of Native Americans decided not to attack. William's Plymouth was safe, at least for a while.

Troubles did come, however, from an unexpected source. When Squanto was around other

Along with Captain Miles Standish, William Bradford helped to lead the Pilgrim army. They wanted to be ready to defend the settlement in case of an attack.

Native Americans, he would pretend that he could make Governor Bradford attack them. He told them that unless they gave him presents, the Englishmen would kill them all with a disease. William wrote that he "began to see that Squanto sought his own end and played his own games . . . and was likely to have cost him his life."

Massasoit did not like Squanto's games. He wanted Squanto dead. For the rest of his life, Squanto had to stay close by the Englishmen because he was afraid Massasoit's people would kill him.

One day, Massasoit sent many braves to Governor Bradford. They asked him to give them Squanto. Governor Bradford didn't want to hand over Squanto. But he also didn't want Massasoit to get angry and attack the Pilgrims. He wanted peace with the Native Americans.

The governor was about to turn in Squanto when someone saw a ship in the bay. William told the braves that before he could do anything about Squanto, he had to see what was on the ship. The braves went away "mad with rage." But Squanto was safe for the time being.

The Pilgrims hoped this was the ship they had been waiting for and that it would have food and supplies. But this ship only brought letters and more hungry people.

In 1622 many boats and ships came and went from Plymouth, and the Pilgrims fed all the passengers. The newcomers did not stay but were going to other towns along the coast.

Because they had been kind and shared their food, the Pilgrims had to live on tiny portions of bread. They began to starve. Some Pilgrims got so hungry they ate corn out of the fields before it was ready for harvest. Governor Bradford had to make sure those people were punished. He didn't want other people to eat all the food they needed for winter.

Finally William got a chance to buy more corn. He and Squanto got on a medium-sized boat with some friends and landed near Cape Cod. They wanted to trade with some Native

In spite of the trouble he caused, Squanto did many things good things for the colonists. Their lives would have been much harder without his help as guide and interpreter.

Americans who had plenty of corn. But the trip was Squanto's last. He got sick and died. The governor wrote that Squanto begged him "to pray for him, that he might go to the Englishmen's God in heaven. . . . His death was a great loss."

At Plimouth Plantation, a modern re-creation of Plymouth colony, visitors get a glimpse of colonial life. These two performers show what the Pilgrims' clothing would have looked like.

The Final
Story

William must have been lonely and tired of living with a bunch of bachelors. There were not many women at Plymouth who were not already married. Where was he to find a wife? A letter came from Holland that said Alice Southworth had become a widow. William remembered Alice from the church at Leyden. He thought she would make a good wife in the wilderness. Both of them were lonely because their spouses had died. He wrote her a letter, asking her to come to Plymouth.

In the summer of 1623, Alice came to America with her two small boys, Thomas and Constant.

When she got off the *Anne,* William was waiting for her. He was probably well dressed, but he was terribly thin. The Pilgrims were practically starving.

The *Anne* brought more than a family for William. This ship came with enough food for its passengers. Without it, many Pilgrims and newcomers would have died.

When William brought Alice to his house, she may have been disappointed. Even being poor in Holland didn't prepare her for the sparse furnishings of William's home. There was only one rug and two silver spoons. Into this humble house, Alice, her two boys, and her sister's family moved.

Those first months of marriage were hard. But Alice Bradford quickly learned that her husband loved the people of Plymouth. As long as they asked him to be governor, he would take the job. She would have to share him.

Alice also knew that raising children was important to William. During their marriage,

Without modern inventions, life in William's time was much harder than it is today. But the Pilgrims' houses were even more sparsely furnished than the homes of many poor people in Europe.

she helped William raise many children, including the three they had together: William Jr., Joseph, and Mercy. There was also John Bradford, William and Dorothy's son, who had finally come from Holland. Alice's own two sons from her first marriage, Thomas and Constant, and her nephew Nathaniel Morton were also part of the household. William and Alice took care of four orphan boys as well. And whenever Alice's family members needed help, William always provided for them.

Years later William Bradford was a happy landowner and family man. He spent many hours teaching all his children how to read and write. He had been chosen as governor by the Plymouth people over and over again. He refused to be paid for the job. He believed that God had given him good things, and he in turn would give to the people.

Mercy, Joseph, and William Jr. heard the stories of Plymouth from their father. There was the time the Saints prayed for rain, and it came down

William and Alice worked hard to provide for their large household. Here some women at Plimouth Plantation demonstrate the preparations for a Pilgrim feast.

To commemorate the 300th anniversary of the Pilgrims' arrival, a plaque in Provincetown, Massachusetts, marks the shore where the Pilgrims first landed, led by (among others) William Bradford.

for two weeks straight. Tales of duels and drunken sailors setting fire to houses were all part of Plymouth's history. William knew his story about

Plymouth should be written down. He called it _Of Plymouth Plantation_. He didn't want people to forget how God had guided the little band of Pilgrims to the New World. In neat handwriting, he wrote down the stories about the Pilgrims. He included many letters from people in Holland and those of the businessmen. It took him twenty years to write it.

It also took a long time to pay back the businessmen. The Plymouth Colony had owed money for a lot more than seven years. In 1648 William Bradford, Captain Standish, and three other men sold a lot of land to pay off the loan. The founders of Plymouth were finally free of debt!

And they were free mostly because of William Bradford's wise choices. As governor, William never thought about himself. He could have made himself a lord over the other people. Instead he made sure that each man got an equal share of land. He made sure that people voted for their leaders so no one person could take over.

When there was very little food to go around, William Bradford made sure that no one starved.

He also kept the church from ruling the people. If Strangers wanted to join the Saints, they were welcomed. But he did not force them to if they chose not to take part in the worship.

> **A Poem by William Bradford**
>
> *From my years young in days of youth,*
> *God did make known to me his truth,*
> *And call'd me from my native place*
> *For to enjoy the means of grace.*
> *In wilderness he did me guide,*
> *And in strange lands for me provide.*
> *In fears and wants, through **weal** and **woe**,*
> *A Pilgrim passed I to and fro.*

William's ideas are some of the best parts of the Pilgrim story. They were the seeds of thought that shaped the government of the United States.

Just before William died in 1657, he was ready to go on another journey. "God has given me a pledge of my happiness in another world," he said. Once again, William was leaving his home to find freedom.

GLOSSARY

Anglican Church official Church of England, run by the English king or queen

compact formal agreement or promise

loom a frame for weaving threads into cloth

martyr someone who is killed for standing up for a strong belief

moat a ring of water that surrounds a building or castle

musket a shoulder gun that is loaded through the muzzle

myth something that most people believe but is not true

Native Americans people who lived in America before Europeans came to settle there

pew a benchlike seat in a church building

port city a city near the water where ships come and go

Puritans religious people in England who wanted to "purify" or change the Church of England

religious freedom the right to worship the way a person believes is correct

Saints the group of Pilgrims who were religious

Separatists religious people in England who wanted to separate from the Church of England

stocks wooden frames made to hold a person by the feet and hands

Strangers the group of Pilgrims who were not religious

weal having happiness and good fortune

woe having sadness and troubles

CHRONOLOGY

1590 William Bradford is born in England.

1602 Bradford joins the Puritan church.

1603 King James begins his rule over England.

1606 Bradford joins the Separatists at Scrooby.

1608 Bradford moves to Holland.

1613 Marries Dorothy May.

1615 John Bradford is born in Holland.

1620 *Mayflower* sets sail for New World in September and arrives at Cape Cod in November. Dorothy Bradford drowns in December at Plymouth.

1621 In April, Bradford is elected governor for the first time. The Pilgrims and the Indians celebrate the first Thanksgiving in October.

1622 Squanto dies.

1623 Bradford marries Alice Southworth.

1624 William Bradford, Jr., is born.

1627 Mercy Bradford is born.

1629 Joseph Bradford is born.

1630–50 Bradford writes *Of Plymouth Plantation*.

1657 William Bradford dies.

COLONIAL TIME LINE

1607 Jamestown, Virginia, is settled by the English.

1620 Pilgrims on the *Mayflower* land at Plymouth, Massachusetts.

1623 The Dutch settle New Netherland, the colony that later becomes New York.

1630 Massachusetts Bay Colony is started.

1634 Maryland is settled as a Roman Catholic colony. Later Maryland becomes a safe place for people with different religious beliefs.

1636 Roger Williams is thrown out of the Massachusetts Bay Colony. He settles Rhode Island, the first colony to give people freedom of religion.

1682 William Penn forms the colony of Pennsylvania.

1688 Pennsylvania Quakers make the first formal protest against slavery.

1692 Trials for witchcraft are held in Salem, Massachusetts.

COLONIAL TIME LINE

1712   Slaves revolt in New York. Twenty-one blacks are killed as punishment.

1720   Major smallpox outbreak occurs in Boston. Cotton Mather and some doctors try a new treatment. Many people think the new treatment shouldn't be used.

1754   French and Indian War begins. It ends nine years later.

1761   Benjamin Banneker builds a wooden clock that keeps precise time.

1765   Britain passes the Stamp Act. Violent protests break out in the colonies. The Stamp Act is ended the next year.

1775   The battles of Lexington and Concord begin the American Revolution.

1776   Declaration of Independence is signed.

FURTHER READING

Bowen, Gary. *Stranded at Plimoth Plantation 1626*. New York: HarperCollins, 1994.

Bradford, William. *Homes in the Wilderness: A Pilgrim's Journal of Plymouth Plantation in 1620,* edited by Margaret Brown. New Haven: Linnet Books, 1988.

Dunnahoo, Terry. *Plimoth Plantation*. Parsippany, N.J.: Dillon Press, 1995.

McGovern, Ann. *If You Sailed on the Mayflower in 1620*. New York: Scholastic, 1991.

Roop, Connie. *Pilgrim Voices: Our First Year in the New World*. New York: Walker & Company Library, 1995.

San Souci, Robert. *N. C. Wyeth's Pilgrims*. San Franciso: Chronicle Books, 1991.

Smith, Bradford. *William Bradford, Pilgrim Boy*. Indianapolis: Bobbs-Merrill, 1953.

Waters, Kate. *Samuel Eaton's Day: A Day in the Life of a Pilgrim Boy*. New York: Scholastic, 1993.

INDEX

INDEX

PICTURE CREDITS

ABOUT THE AUTHORS

MARIANNE KENDRICK HERING has written hundreds of magazine articles for children's magazines. This is her eighth book for young people. Her daughter, Danielle, age eight, thinks it's the best one yet.

Senior Consulting Editor **ARTHUR M. SCHLESINGER, JR.** is the leading American historian of our time. He won the Pulitzer Prize for his book *The Age of Jackson* (1945) and again for *A Thousand Days* (1965). This chronicle of the Kennedy Administration also won a National Book Award. He has written many other books including a multi-volume series, *The Age of Roosevelt*. Professor Schlesinger is the Albert Schweitzer Professor of the Humanities at the City University of New York, and has been involved in several other Chelsea House projects, including the REVOLUTIONARY WAR LEADERS biographies on the most prominent figures of early American history.

jB
BRADFORD

Hering, Marianne.

William Bradford,
governor of Plymouth
Colony.

$18.95

DATE			